Wine Cellars

An Exploration of Stylish Storage

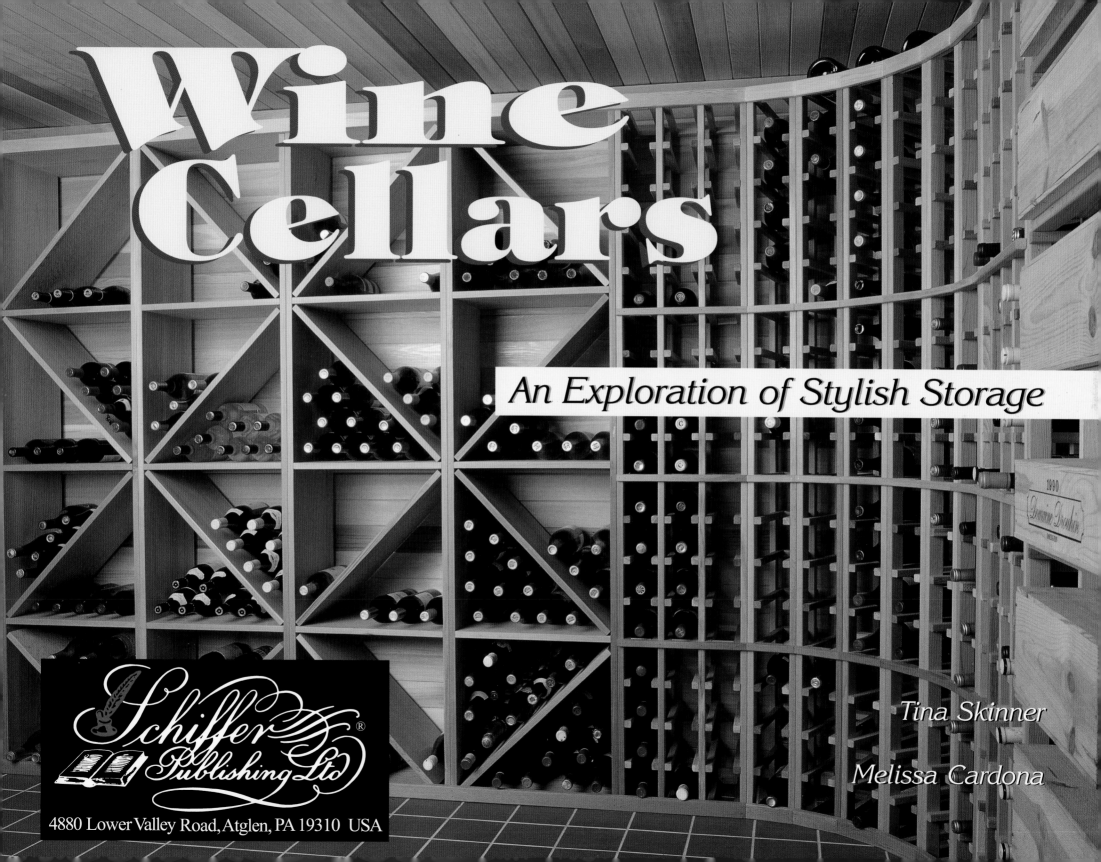

Wine Cellars

An Exploration of Stylish Storage

Schiffer Publishing Ltd

4880 Lower Valley Road, Atglen, PA 19310 USA

Tina Skinner

Melissa Cardona

Acknowledgments

This book has been a labor of passion. The people whose work is shown, and those interviewed, are simply not out to make a buck. This is an all-consuming interest, a subject peopled by enthusiasts. Eminent among the talents pooled for this publication is Paul Wyatt, whose incredible 3D vision created many of the wine cellars shown, and whose talented eye extended to photography, capturing many of the inspiring images within these covers. Many thanks to Paul, and the other designers whose work is sure to ignite the passion to build and acquire!

Library of Congress Cataloging-in-Publication Data

Skinner, Tina.
  Wine cellars : an exploration of stylish storage / by Tina Skinner, Melissa Cardona.
    p. cm.
  ISBN 0-7643-1965-5
1. Wine cellars. I. Cardona, Melissa. II. Title.
TP548.5.A6 S54 2004
641.2'2--dc22

2003020841

Designed by Mark David Bowyer
Type set in Tiffany Hv BT / Korinna BT

ISBN: 0-7643-1965-5
Printed in China

Published by Schiffer Publishing Ltd.
4880 Lower Valley Road
Atglen, PA 19310
Phone: (610) 593-1777; Fax: (610) 593-2002
E-mail: Info@schifferbooks.com

For the largest selection of fine reference books on this and related subjects, please visit our web site at
www.schifferbooks.com
We are always looking for people to write books on new and related subjects. If you have an idea for a book please contact us at the above address.

This book may be purchased from the publisher.
Include $3.95 for shipping.
Please try your bookstore first.
You may write for a free catalog.

In Europe, Schiffer books are distributed by
Bushwood Books
6 Marksbury Ave.
Kew Gardens
Surrey TW9 4JF England
Phone: 44 (0) 20 8392-8585; Fax: 44 (0) 20 8392-9876
E-mail: info@bushwoodbooks.co.uk
Free postage in the U.K., Europe; air mail at cost.

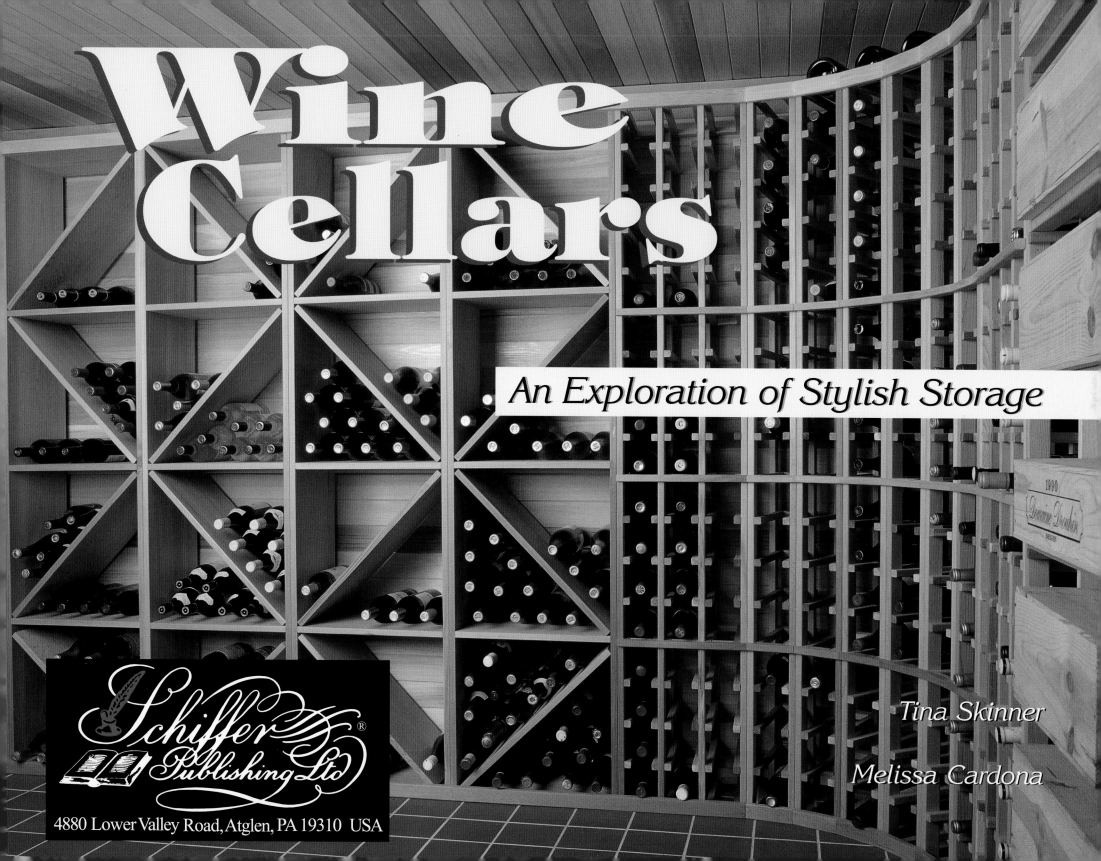

Wine Cellars

An Exploration of Stylish Storage

Tina Skinner

Melissa Cardona

Schiffer Publishing Ltd.

4880 Lower Valley Road, Atglen, PA 19310 USA

Acknowledgments

This book has been a labor of passion. The people whose work is shown, and those interviewed, are simply not out to make a buck. This is an all-consuming interest, a subject peopled by enthusiasts. Eminent among the talents pooled for this publication is Paul Wyatt, whose incredible 3D vision created many of the wine cellars shown, and whose talented eye extended to photography, capturing many of the inspiring images within these covers. Many thanks to Paul, and the other designers whose work is sure to ignite the passion to build and acquire!

Library of Congress Cataloging-in-Publication Data

Skinner, Tina.
  Wine cellars : an exploration of stylish storage / by Tina Skinner, Melissa Cardona.
    p. cm.
  ISBN 0-7643-1965-5
1. Wine cellars. I. Cardona, Melissa. II. Title.
TP548.5.A6 S54 2004
641.2'2--dc22

2003020841

Designed by Mark David Bowyer
Type set in Tiffany Hv BT / Korinna BT

ISBN: 0-7643-1965-5
Printed in China

Published by Schiffer Publishing Ltd.
4880 Lower Valley Road
Atglen, PA 19310
Phone: (610) 593-1777; Fax: (610) 593-2002
E-mail: Info@schifferbooks.com

For the largest selection of fine reference books on this and related subjects, please visit our web site at
www.schifferbooks.com
We are always looking for people to write books on new and related subjects. If you have an idea for a book please contact us at the above address.

This book may be purchased from the publisher.
Include $3.95 for shipping.
Please try your bookstore first.
You may write for a free catalog.

In Europe, Schiffer books are distributed by
Bushwood Books
6 Marksbury Ave.
Kew Gardens
Surrey TW9 4JF England
Phone: 44 (0) 20 8392-8585; Fax: 44 (0) 20 8392-9876
E-mail: info@bushwoodbooks.co.uk
Free postage in the U.K., Europe; air mail at cost.

Contents

Introduction

There is a revolution underway in the world of beverages. Wine is finding a home on the palates of a growing wine-loving public. These increasingly educated wine fans are interested in experiencing quality wines, and understanding their experience.

Expert wine production has moved from a few exclusive provinces in France and Italy to all points East and West as "flying winemakers" have disseminated their centuries-old knowledge to far flung grape growers and vintners. Wine regions are cropping up all over "new world" countries such as the United States, South Africa, Australia, and New Zealand. Winery tours, tasting programs, and wine appreciation courses are becoming standard vacation fare for middle class epicureans.

To keep up, and to cash in, restaurants are actively enhancing their "wine programs," promoting wines along with the more traditional mixed drinks and beer. Staff is being trained to make customers more comfortable. Restaurants are luring customers with ads that prominently feature toasting wine goblets, or by presenting special wine programs to solicit reservations for pricey five-course meals.

Moreover, subscriber numbers are soaring for several magazines dedicated solely to the business and pleasure of wine. Plus, consumers are apt to create their own wine journals or diaries dedicated to their experiences with wine.

But this is all old news. The *real* news is buried deep beneath people's homes. The crème de la crème of wine connoisseurs are beefing up their personal wine programs, and discovering in wine both pleasure and potential financial investment. By buying young and aging properly, they're providing themselves with top quality wines, and a much more valuable and marketable commodity. It's a habit that can pay for itself.

In addition, for the up and coming, a wine cellar is certainly a one-up on the Joneses. You can get a bit more than a nickel for the house tour when there's a wine cellar downstairs.

This book is not intended as the be-all, end-all of wine storage techniques. Many other resources are available on that subject. Instead, this is a vicarious tour of an incredible selection of wine cellars—a beautiful dream book that raises the bar on that basement closet where a few cases lie in dusty disrespect. It's an opportunity to dream, plan, and plot that perfect, climate-controlled, mouth-watering display of your own future collection.

Enjoy!

An entrance characterized by glass doors and segmental arches makes a graceful transition between the tiled wine cellar and carpeted hallway.

A fish-eye lens provides an interesting perspective on this gorgeous wine cellar.

11

Glass shelves in a decorative opening increase display space.

A 1920s French champagne Ridling rack. This kind of rack is still in use today.

14

Curved racking and elaborate display areas distinguish the private dining room of Don Carano below the Italian Palazio at Ferrari Carano. Painted ceiling and color-swirled flooring provide an earthy setting for wrought iron chairs and table, watched over by a robust hanging lamp.

A step inside the high end wine tasting room off the main floor at Ferrari Carano affords a trip into the Tuscan countryside. Wine just tastes better when sipped among the scenery provided by a magnificent mural, which invites the viewer to walk along an arbor vitae path. Faux marble columns and an arched ceiling add even more distinction to the space.

Tile patterns on the floor match the curve of
the racks in this 3,000 bottle cellar. Small
display shelves are used to hold bottles and
display favorite pictures. A refrigeration unit
is mounted flush to a display cabinet with a
glass door and soft lighting.

Bottles of fine wine climb their
way up a stair-like racking
system, providing extra storage
without cramping a small space.
Slate tile flooring and a hanging
lamp are nice decorative features.

Marble flooring and cherry wood racking with convex curved display shelves make an ordinary basement an extraordinary wine storage space. Vents above the racks provide air circulation for the hi-tech temperature control system. A painting in the decorative opening and a wine cask on the floor enhance the refined look of this wine cellar.

Stone creates a rustic appeal, reminiscent of the French caves where wine was traditionally stored. The hardwood ceiling and floor add red warmth to the gray, cool tone of the stone, while the stemware and bottle seals add bright bursts of color. A decorative opening features a primitive-looking stone sculpture.

Not quite sure what to do with all those corks? Use them for decorative purposes! The owners of this wine cellar add a creative and personal touch with this "wreath" made of corks.

Why Cellar Wine?

Wine wasn't always cellared. In fact, the ancient Romans rushed to finish their wine as soon as a batch ripened. Their experience taught them that, if they kept it too long it would spoil.

The art of aging wines was developed deep in French caves, where wine makers discovered that time could improve wines' flavor, aroma, and complexity.

Done correctly, cellaring protects a wine from spoilage by environmental stresses such as temperature fluctuations, dryness, light, and even odors. Wine storage is every bit as important as a wine's ingredients and preparation.

In fact, for those who appreciate the subtle nuances of drinking wine, storage is everything. Beyond that, there's a financial motive to properly cellaring wine. Wine is an increasingly popular investment, having entered the arena of antiques. Major auction houses now handle wines, as do online auctions. *Newsweek* provides a weekly column advising readers of good wine purchases. And financial sections of newspapers include articles about wine as a healthy investment.

In the trade, restaurants and hotel chains often buy wines young, and in massive quantity, in order to increase the resale value of the product at a later date. Consumers do the same on a smaller scale. It's all speculative, but profitable for the informed.

Wine cellaring takes patience. A fine wine takes at least two years to mature. The wise consumer buys wines as they are released, then tucks them away carefully. Great vintages can be purchased before they mature, when their prices skyrocket. Many people buy by the case and, when the wine reaches maturity, sell half and drink half for free.

It is an addictive pursuit that can pay for itself, or one that may simply pay off in many hours of shared enjoyment over a fine wine.

The arched doorway and tile flooring give a subtle European flavor to this wine cellar. A tile countertop provides practicality in addition to style.

This three level cellar
with bridge and
"KOA" slab counter
provides the perfect
space to enjoy
crackers and cheese
with a glass of wine.

Rope lighting and display angle racking in three sizes make a beautiful and practical combination.

This luminous wine cellar features tile flooring with a mosaic border. Large bottles cradled in horizontal racks entice dinner parties eating at the spectacular table.

A lounge area creates the perfect casual gathering place. Here, after a bottle has been selected from the climate-controlled storage room beyond, it can be uncorked and savored at leisure in comfortable chairs.

A Gothic style entrance opens up to a grotto-like cellar. The floor is made of natural rock formations that were original to the basement and incorporated into the design of the wine cellar.

A corner cabinet creates an enclosure for the less sightly items stored in this cellar and hides a lump in the basement floor.

Proper Construction

"Building it right the first time"

By Doug M. Smith,
Owner, Apex Wine Cellars & Racking

I can't tell you how many times I've talked with wine collectors over the years who cut corners during the construction phase, and had problems with the function of their cellar soon after they put their first bottles into the racks. They all wished they had *"built it right the first time."* The common theme is that either they never spent the time to research how to prepare the cellar, or they simply refused to listen to the advice of a qualified wine cellar consultant, often not wanting to spend the extra money. In most cases, fixing the problem requires removal of all your wine, removing the racking that is attached to the walls, and removing the drywall or wood paneling to get into the walls to repair the problem. The result is that you spend far more money to do it twice than doing it correctly just once.

Wine cellars are not everyday products that are installed into homes. Architects and builders just do not have enough experience to fully understand the

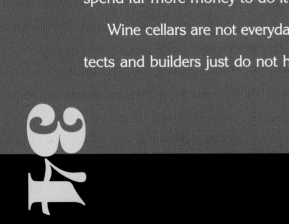

fine construction details needed to make sure your valuable wine collection is properly stored. It is always recommended that you hire a qualified wine cellar consultant to make sure you are doing it right. To give you some basic assistance, below are some useful tips to make sure the cellar is built right.

Wall & Ceiling Framing: Build your wine cellar walls using standard 2 x 4 or 2 x 6 construction methods and ceiling joists, and follow the guidelines of local and state codes in your area. The general rule for a cellar is that the thicker the walls, and the better the insulation factor, the better the cellar remains at a consistent temperature.

Vapor Barrier: A vapor barrier is required if a climate control cooling unit is installed to keep the cellar at the correct temperature. 6-mill plastic sheeting is applied to the *hot* side of the cellar walls. All walls and the ceiling must be wrapped in plastic for a complete vapor barrier.

Insulation: Insulation is required on the walls and ceiling of a cellar. Standard "Fiberglass" or "Rigid Foam" insulation is normally used in cellar construction. Blown in insulation or liquid foam that hardens can also be used. It is very important that all walls and ceiling be insulated to keep the cellar temperature as consistent as possible during the summer and winter months.

Wall & Ceiling Coverings: The interior wall and ceiling covering is determined by the décor theme of the cellar. Often drywall (green board) is applied, and then painted (always use latex paint) to match a color theme of the cellar. It is also very common to apply wood paneling material to the walls and/or ceiling of a cellar. This paneling is normally the same wood species as the racking material that makes for a very uniform look throughout the cellar. Stone or granite is also used as a wall covering material.

Cellar Doors: An exterior grade (1-3/4") door must be installed as a cellar door. It is very important that weather stripping is attached to all four sides of the doorjamb. A bottom "sweep" or threshold is also needed. The door

must have a very good seal to keep the cool cellar air from escaping out of the cellar. One of the most common problems with cooling units running continually is due to not sealing the door properly. Solid core doors or doors with a full glass insert are most often used. Glass doors must have at least double pane, tempered glass.

Climate Controlled Systems: All the room preparations described above are very important. You can follow these instructions to the last detail, but if you do not choose the proper cooling equipment your cellar will not maintain the proper temperature and humidity levels. Thus your valuable wine collection could be permanently harmed. A cellar must keep a temperature of about 53-58 degrees and humidity of 50-70 percent. There are several types of cooling equipment. Some of the criteria we use to determine which cooling equipment to use are size and layout of your cellar, the number of bottles to be stored, your geographic region of the country, direction of the sun hitting exterior walls, glass doors or window, etc. You will need to consult with an expert who can specify the correct cooling system because there is no simple way to size units yourself.

Some lovely features of this wine cellar include tiered racking, a decorative opening with shelving and mirror-backing, and a gorgeous window with stained glass accent. A cushioned bench was fashioned from wine storage boxes and backed by an elaborate wrought iron gate. A beautiful storage armoire with glass cabinets adds a magnificent and creative touch.

Opposite: Amazing how a mere faux grape vine adds so much life to this wine cellar. A hanging light fixture provides distinction. Above: A marvelous stone floor perfectly complements the racking in this cellar. Racks climb like stairs to the ceiling, effectively occupying the open space of the room. A practical table with a circular end and quarter round shelves juts out of the racks. This smart feature provides extra storage space for case boxes underneath and an ideal spot to select and taste wine.

Wine cellars aren't just for wine. Multiple display and storage options give this wine cellar versatility, while adding beauty and interesting detail. There is space for stemware, art, and spirits.

Paul Wyatt's old showroom
in San Carlos, California
features tiered box-racking
topped with display space
— a smart and stylish way
to store large bottles.
Lighting accentuates and
adds depth to the cellar.
Good taste doesn't only
apply to wine: an arched
decorative opening with
backlighting features a
graceful, bronze Basso
sculpture.

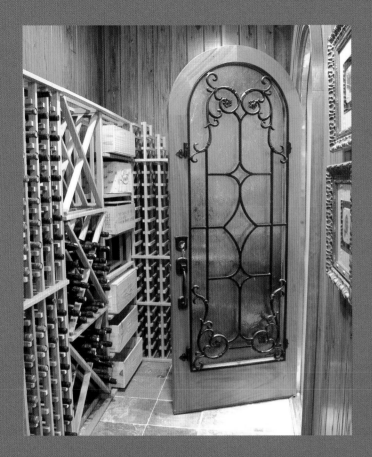

Flagstone flooring and wood paneling characterize this new wine cellar, ripe for stocking. Beyond is a dining and lounge area where most guests gather. However, for those who want to enjoy cigars, the cellar itself has been reserved for smoking. Lest the cigars create thirst, there are liquors in addition to the household stock in wine.

An exquisite, glass-enclosed table area allows guests to admire the wine collection without affecting the cellar's climate. Sand-blasted decoration on glass enhances the beauty of this room. Be wary of carpeted floors, as they may develop mold in the preferably humid conditions of a wine cellar.

Temperature

Wine is like a living, breathing organism. It interacts with its environment, vulnerable to conditions over which it has no control. Thankfully, however, you do.

A seemingly inert bottle of wine undergoes hundreds of chemical reactions, desirable to oenophiles only if they occur under the right conditions. These same chemical reactions can very easily become a collector's worst enemy. Temperature is the principle determining factor of how and to what degree these chemical reactions take place, thus the importance of strict temperature control in a wine cellar.

Customarily, a constant 55°F (13°C) is the ideal temperature at which to store wine. Some sources claim that this value stems from the temperature of the caves where wine was traditionally stored in France. Different experts assert that temperatures ranging from 50°F to 60°F are acceptable as long as the temperature remains constant. Frequent and rapid fluctuations in temperature can be detrimental to the proper aging of wine. For example, wine can easily be ruined during transport; just one hour in a hot trunk can produce the same amount of chemical reactions that occur over weeks in a properly stored bottle.

Storing wine at the ideal temperature allows it to undergo chemical reactions at a rate that produces desirable changes in composition and flavor. Chemical reactions occur with more frequency as temperatures rise, aging wine more and more rapidly at higher values. Not only will higher temperatures age wine more quickly, they may produce undesirable chemical reactions that occur with less frequency, or not at all, at lower temperatures. Some of the unfavorable effects of heat damage include an unpleasant taste or odor, premature browning, or a brick edge in young wine. While storing wine at temperatures cooler than the ideal 55°F may not necessarily destroy wine, it will retard wine's maturation process, which occurs at values above 40°F. In addition, lower temperatures may lead to deposits or suspensions in wine.

A wine cellar is a like an ecosystem, constantly in flux; like the wine that it stores, it is susceptible to the effects of the environment that surrounds it. During summer months, heat can flow into a cellar through the ceiling, adjacent basement rooms, and the soil. A cellar's climate can be affected by even an hour's worth of breath, a door left ajar, or a light left turned on. Proper climate control measures are imperative to the success of any wine cellar, and represent the most important component in a cellar's construction.

No expense should be spared when it comes to a cellar's climate control system. Its effectiveness will ultimately determine the quality of the finest vintages, which can very easily turn foul under the wrong conditions. Good insulation is a must, as is good planning. Cellars buried deep beneath the ground are less subject to wild fluctuations in atmospheric temperature, which make artificial climate systems work twice as hard. The possibility of a power outage during the dead heat of summer must also be taken into consideration. Just a few hours spent in excessive heat can damage wine, so collectors must constantly remain on guard.

Here are some proper wine storage options for homes with limited space. Rather than compromising style for utility, these self-contained wine cellars housed in fine wood credenzas and tall cabinets enhance the look of living areas.

This sleek, full-height wine cooler holds up to 150 bottles. Elegant and attractive, the built-in cooler provides the perfect option for wine storage in homes without the space for a wine cellar. Some "cool" features include three independent temperature zones, vibration-reducing shelves, and ultraviolet resistant glass.

15

A stone wall that curves from one counter to another adds texture to this bar area, featuring diagonal racking, a refrigeration unit, and a bottle-lined wallpaper border.

Originally an aging wine cask for fine vintages, this cooler is a creative and stylish way to keep beverages cool for parties. It features wrought-iron legs, a spring-hinged top with a lock, and a spout for easy drainage. The tasting stools are also made from oak aging barrels and wrought iron.

While serving as an island countertop between kitchen and dining areas, this wine storage cabinet is temperature and humidity controlled to perfectly preserve its valuable contents.

This Georgian style English chest was fitted to hold the sixty-one bottle 1855 Classified Growth set.

No need to travel far from the dinner table for a fine selection of wine. A wine racking system installed into the wall is a simple and elegant method for wine storage.

A small selection of wine is kept handy in the kitchen. Blue countertops and ceilings colorfully offset the white cabinets in this cozy kitchen. Far right: Cabinetry with molding and special wine storage combines delightfully with a white tile backdrop featuring geometric designs in blue and rust. Flowers add beauty and life to any space.

A dining area features a practical built-in wine rack and cabinet space.

Wood

After climate control, the most important component in wine cellar construction is probably the racking system responsible for holding bottles. Wood, and more specifically, redwood, has long been a favored material used by racking manufacturers and cellar engineers. Wood's beauty, availability, versatility, and durability make it an optimal building material for use in such systems.

The popularity of redwood in wine cellar applications traditionally stems from the practice of wine-making in Northern California, where redwood trees grow in abundance and were used to make wine vats, barrels, bottle racks, and just about every other construction for which wood was useful. Charlie Jourdain, wood technologist with the California Redwood Association, says that apart from its abundance, redwood is a great material to use in cellaring wines due to its excellent strength-

to-weight ratio, decay and shock resistance, easy workability, and insulating properties. Another advantage of using redwood is that it can be left untreated —its warm and glowing natural beauty eliminates the need to use any finishes or stains.

Supplies of high grade old-growth redwood have dwindled and costs of these grades have risen in recent years due to restrictions placed on harvesting of private lands by the state of California. As with other kinds of wood, redwood comes in different grades, with "Clear All Heart" redwood being the most expensive and most attractive. The only real difference between Clear All Heart and more economical grades like B Grade is in appearance, and has little to do with the actual quality of the wood.

Paul Wyatt, of the Napa, California based Fine Wine Rack and Cellar Company, says that fundamentally, there is little difference in the func-

though, given that there are less aromatic varieties like the western red cedar, which is a common building material.

Proper functionality should be a concern when choosing a wood variety for wine racks, but in essence, the pure aesthetics of a racking system are what matter most. As long as a good climate control system is installed, there should be no need to worry about the decay-resistant properties of naturally durable wood species. More important than the wood used to build a wine racking system is the quality of the racking system's construction. There should be plenty of air flow between the racks to prevent moisture buildup, and they should be built to fit the needs of a collector who stores regular bottles, magnums, and cases of wine.

In summary, a wine cellar should be beautiful. It should be shown off to friends. Function without form is no fun, so proper care should be given to ensure that the racking system complements the overall style of the cellar. Your investment should be protected, but why not enjoy it in the meantime?

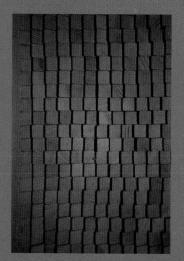

Redwood emanates beauty in addition to providing an ideal building material for high-humidity applications. A turn-of-the-century root cellar is transformed by arched doorways, redwood paneling and floors, and prefabricated wine racks encased with redwood boards to give a custom-built look. Redwood-encased ceiling pipes and ducts further beautify this basement.

67

A table built with wine rack units and topped with redwood planks provides a robust space for wine tasting and extra storage space.

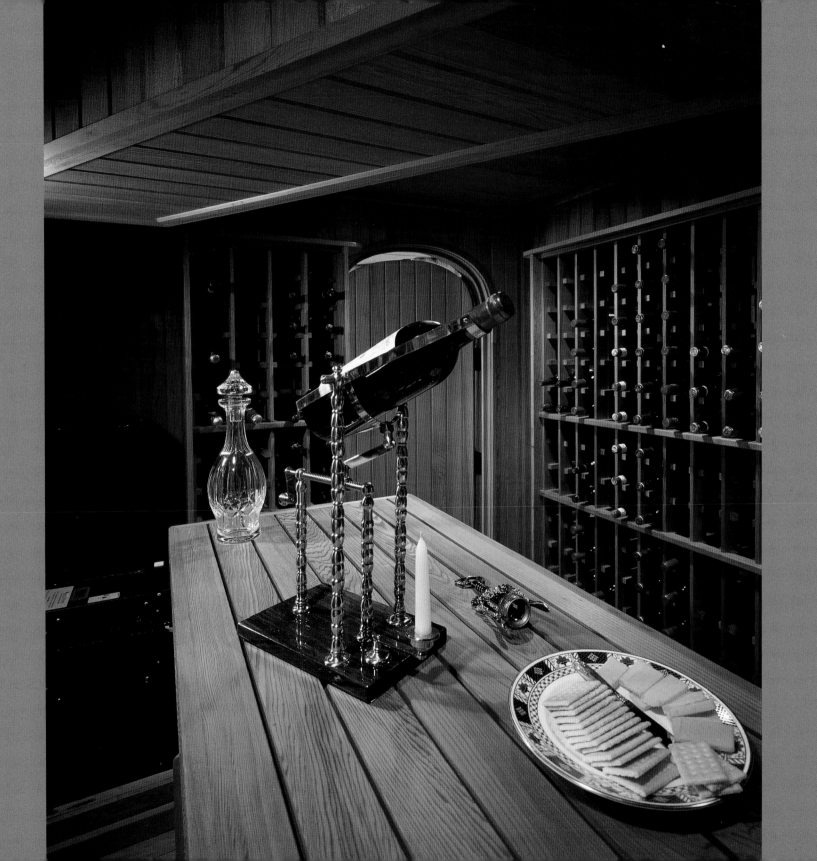

71

Curved corner and overhead racking take advantage of every inch – practical and pretty. Tile flooring, decorative opening with mirror, and quarter round shelves add pretty finishing touches.

Look at those curves! Rounded racks and arching doorways make straight spaces more appeal-ing. La Bruschetta in Westwood, California.

Humidity

The aging of fine wine is an intricate process, requiring the harmonious balance of numerous interrelated factors. If this balance is neglected, an unfavorable combination of the components can adversely affect the quality of vintage wine. One of the many concerns when cellaring wine is the relative humidity level of its storage area. Humidity levels that are too high can result in the growth of mold, which ruins wood, cork stoppers, labels, and other paper surfaces. On the other hand, collectors must worry about corks drying out and excessive evaporation of wine in drier spaces.

The rapid growth of mold occurs at relative humidity levels of 80% or more. Especially for those who actually cellar in the cellar, late spring and early summer offer the greatest threat of high humidity and mold development. Although high humidity levels do not affect wine directly, that hard-to-get-rid-of mold can ruin a gorgeous cellar and destroy the labels of the most highly prized and coveted vintages. After all, the pleasure derived from a fine vintage comes not only from its palatable consumption, but also from the satisfaction reaped when guests' turn their gazes toward a thirty-year-old bottle and approvingly inspect its label.

In terms of maintaining the quality of wine, collectors should be more concerned about the deleterious effects of *low* humidity levels, which dry out corks and increase rates of evaporation. Excess amounts of oxygen-rich air replace precious drops of fine vintages during the evaporation process and destroy them through premature aging. During the winter months, one must remain especially alert, as the moisture capacity of air decreases with temperature. Of course, even wines in the best of care will suffer minor levels of evaporation and develop some ullage, but collectors must be very careful lest their favorite vintages virtually disappear and age before their time. Storing bottles on their sides is a preventive measure to keep corks from drying out; however, one must still take care to ensure that the air side of the cork is protected from low humidity levels.

Impeccably good taste means nothing if accompanied by disregard and negligence in the care of stored wine. The best way to avoid an embarrassing and disappointing wine inauguration is to take careful precautions in the construction of a wine cellar. Any effort and resources applied at the start of a wine cellar project to ensure proper humidity

levels will more than compensate for themselves by safeguarding your wine assets in the future. Careful monitoring will also prove invaluable in the long run. Any serious collector should invest in a hydrometer to measure the relative humidity level of a cellar, even if the cellar already comes equipped with a sophisticated climate control system. Relative humidity levels can vary greatly in the smallest of spaces, a condition that generates the need to measure the humidity levels of multiple places in the same cellar. Acceptable relative humidity levels fall between 60 and 80%.

One can never be too careful when it comes to fine wine, which constantly comes under assault by the elements. Wine is sensitive to even the most minor fluctuations in environmental factors, just as relative humidity levels are subject to significant change as a result of variations in the atmospheric conditions of a cellar. Simply breathing in a cellar releases water vapor into the air, as does burning a candle or breaking a bottle of wine. The moral of humidity's story is to constantly remain aware of the conditions in your cellar. The effort employed now will save much grief and frustration in the future.

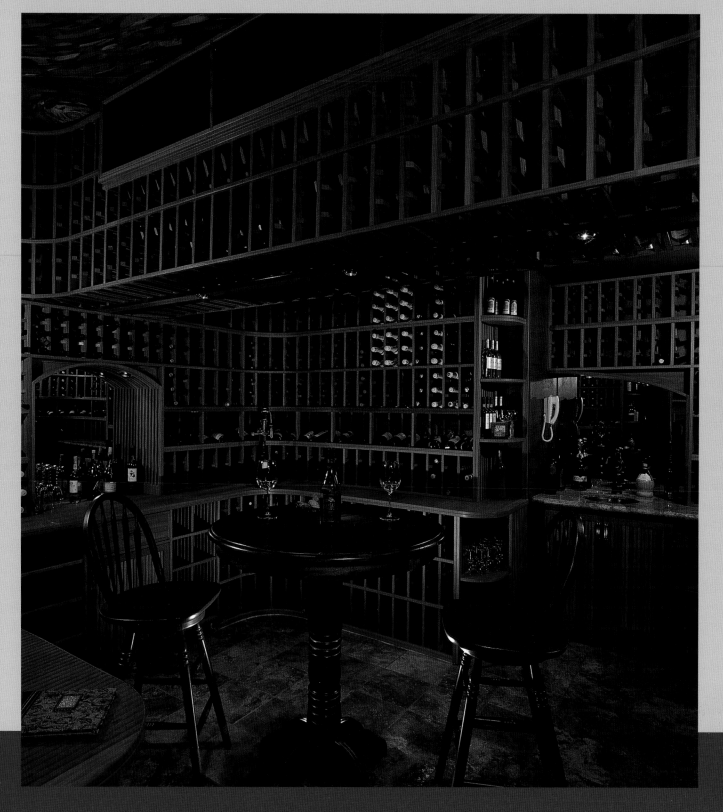

The sandblasted marble floor and painted ceiling give the impression of being under water. Guests can look up and see fishes near the surface. The wine cellar's ship-like décor complements the ocean theme. Jarrah wood racks hold about 4,000 bottles.

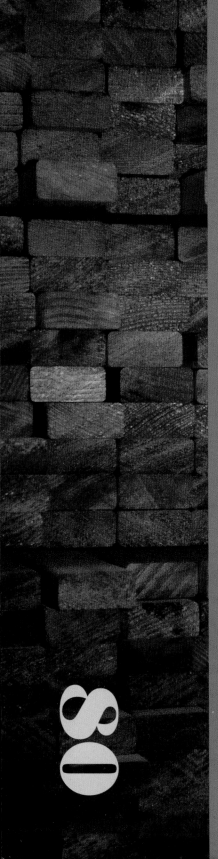

A painting features cherubs climbing a beam of light emitted from a bottle of wine.

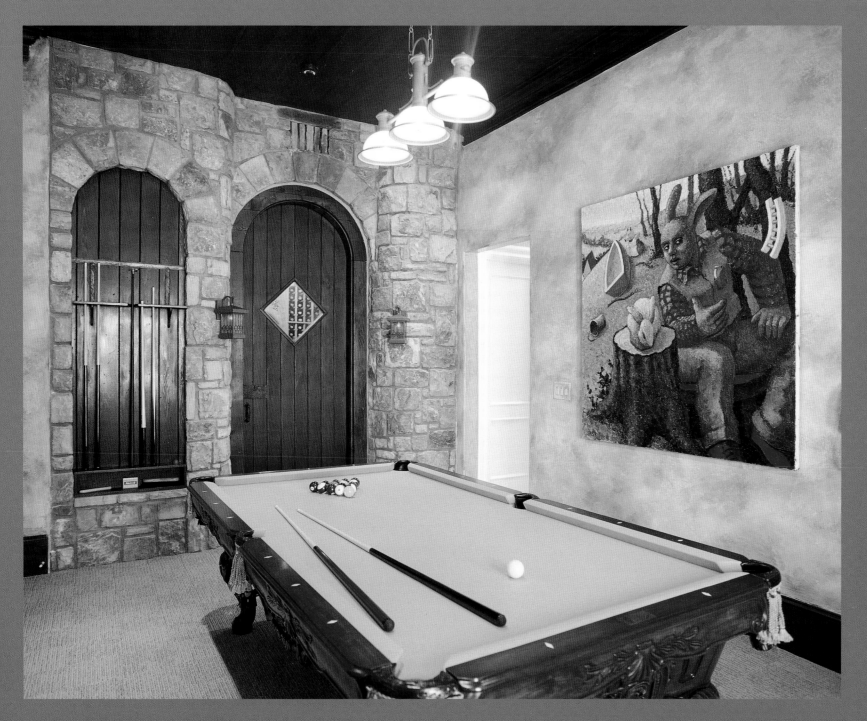

A billiards table occupies the center of a room that leads into the wine cellar. The bright painting and sponged walls add warmth to the room. Guillotine cut limestone and fieldstone create a rustic feel. Inside, the fully stocked wine cellar boasts an interlocking terra-cotta floor and a beautiful painting of a wine country scene. Grapevine accents above arched doorways add color and character.

Sandblasted decoration and lettering on a glass doorway contribute class to the entrance of this library wine cellar. Walls without racking open up the room and achieve extra style with circular mirror and wine posters for adornments.

A vine motif was stenciled on the floor to add décor to this working wine cellar, where the walls have been fully racked to maximize storage space, including every inch under the tasting table. Opposite page: Part of Bressler Vinyards' 9,000 bottle cellar in St. Helena, California.

Arch trim fascia over a decorative opening provides a beautiful focal point in this wine cellar. The simple yet elegant break in wine racks affords a place to display the key bottle to the case collection above or below. The marble floor, central island, and display "rope lighting" on individual bottle racking are other special features of this cellar. Opposite page: Wine cellars aren't just for storing wine! Hanging stemware racks and a decorative opening with back lighting provide the perfect place to enjoy wine with guests.

Light

Among the many dangers that threaten aging wine, light is another potential enemy. Ultraviolet light induces chemical reactions that can cause hydrogen sulphide compounds to develop in wine—affecting the wine's aroma, flavor, and structure—and can also promote premature aging. Another undesirable effect of light is the onset of copper haze, or *cupric casse* in white wines.

Although the look of natural light is preferable in any space, for optimum storage conditions, windows should not be included in the design of a wine cellar. If this cannot be avoided, however, UV resistant windows are available. Otherwise, be sure to keep the windows shaded from the sun or the wine stored away from the light.

In addition to the potential dangers of natural light, one must also consider the effects of artificial lighting systems on wine. Installing a lighting system is an important aspect of wine cellar construction and informed choices can prevent problems in the future. In general, lights with low wattage are probably the best choice for a wine cellar because strong light can promote some wine diseases. Fluorescent light is typically not a good choice for wine cellar applications because it emits UV rays. Collectors should also be wary of incandescent lights that produce a lot of heat and can significantly increase the temperature of a wine cellar. If using recessed lighting, extra caution should be taken with the installation, as improper installation can allow heat and humidity leaks.

Good habits and conscientious use of lights can offset some of the dangers of light to wine. Lights should never be left on for extended periods of time. As long as lights are consistently used sparingly, any kind of light will do. There are certain preventive measures one can take to ensure that lights are not left on unwittingly. One option includes installing lights that run on a timer. Another includes the installation of an indicator light, usually red, or an alarm that will serve as a reminder that the wine cellar lights have been left on.

Wine in clear bottles is most susceptible to the effects of UV light. While dark or green bottles do offer more protection, they do not prevent the onset of "lightstruck" flavors that result from light-induced chemical reactions. White or sparkling wines are most sensitive to light, and should be stored in the darkest part of a cellar.

As with other dangers to wine, the undesirable effects of light can be avoided through careful planning and attention.

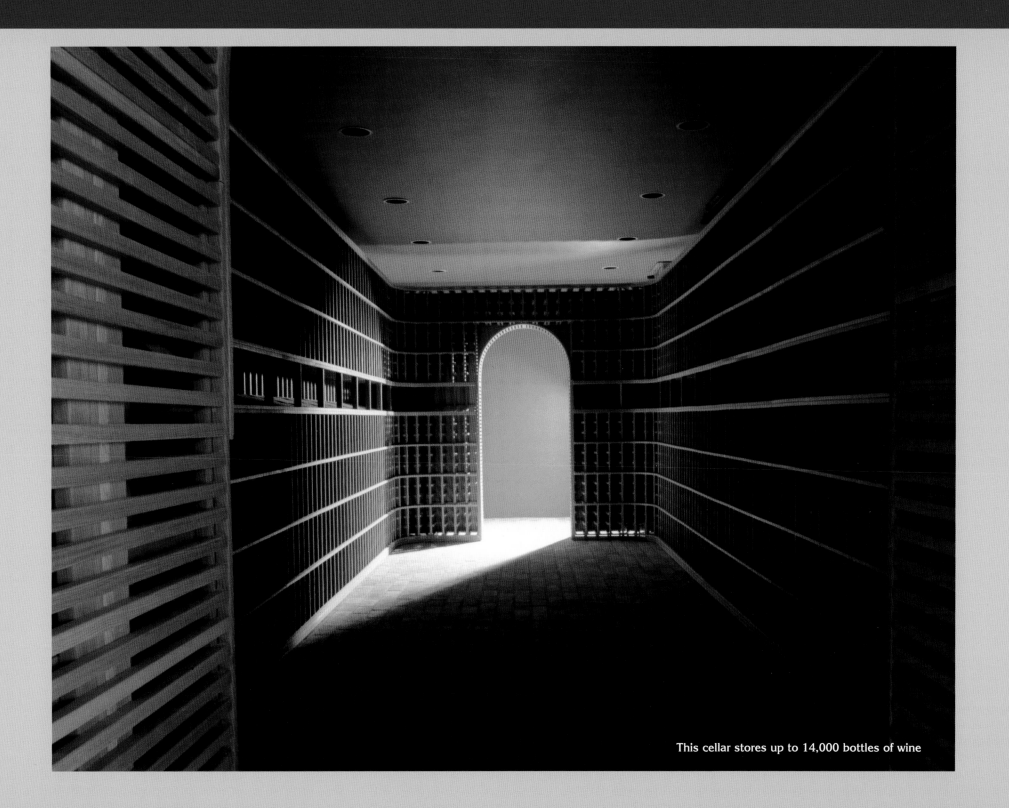

This cellar stores up to 14,000 bottles of wine

A custom design ceiling panel creates the impression of a skylight, adding a one-of-a-kind design element to this cellar.

Dark green walls frame diagonal bins and accent the earthy tile flooring in this room. Light pours in through a large window overlooking an outdoor entrance. Some communal wine cellars rent out private storage lockers like those found above the bins. Opposite page: Multiple racking features complement each other gracefully, while stone tile and candlelight exude a rustic quality.

Rope lighting adds character to a decorative opening.

96

A mirrored corner bar area amplifies light and space, and the photographer.

The stained glass lamp above the circular table, pastel-colored painting, and the floral print upholstered chairs make this wine cellar feel as cozy as a kitchen.

Rope lighting adds character to decorative openings.

Friends can enjoy sipping wine together in a cellar like this one. Tiers of box-racking and an overhead bridge offset the table area nicely, while rows of recessed lighting flank a barrel-vaulted ceiling.

Utility and style go hand in hand. A V-shaped island provides extra storage and display space while creating the perfect nook for a wine-tasting table.

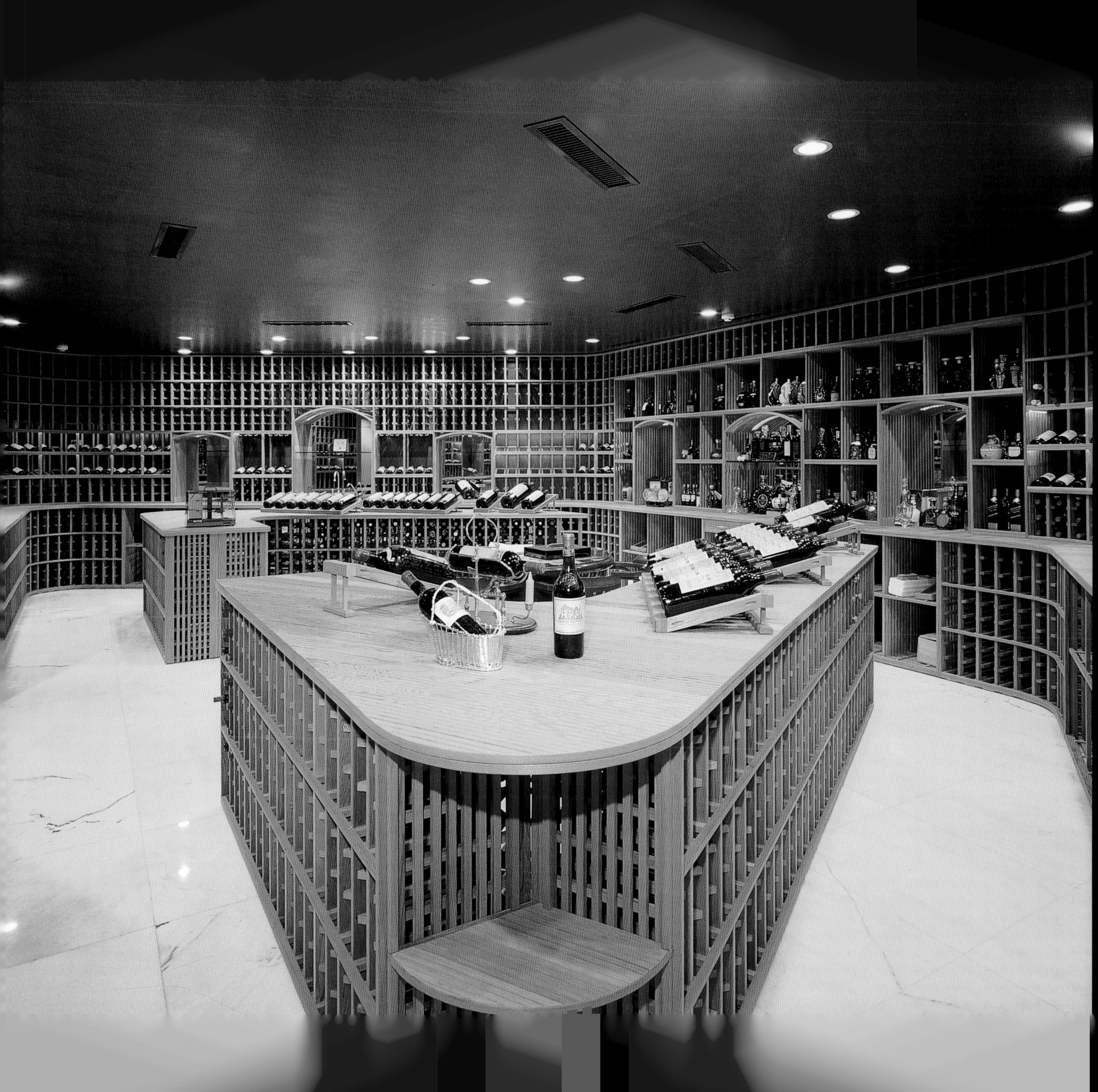

In an age-old trick, a designer has incorporated diagonal lines in the central table to create an impression of width in the room. This helps in a space where one is seated amidst towering racks on all sides.

Decorative openings with mirror backing and plenty of display racking lend versatility to the look of this wine cellar. Light marble flooring opens up the room, giving the appearance of more space.

A brightly colored mural and tile flooring with decorative paintings make this room ripe with color. The stair-like rack with an inclining top shelf seems to slide right into the rows of vines in the painting behind it. The slanting recessed display areas above the painting are unique to this cellar.

Vibration

There is no consensus among the experts about the effects of vibration on wine. Some claim that excessive vibration can affect the aging process, while others say that its effects are only of concern just prior to consumption.

Vibration occurs in noisy areas, anywhere near running motors, and storage spaces close to roads. Refrigeration units are also prone to vibrate under the influence of their motors, and many of these are marketed as containing vibration-resistant shelves.

Although it is not known for certain whether vibration affects wine's chemical processes, vibration does stir up the contents of aging wine and hinders the settling of sediments. In order to ensure that wine has settled properly, one should simply stand a bottle up several days before consumption. Richard M. Gold, in *How and Why to Build a Wine Cellar*, recommends placing a bottle in a 45° angled wine stand to compact the sediment to one side of the bottle and decanting before serving without placing the bottle upright. Sediments do not taste good, and their presence in a glass can ruin any properly aged vintage.

Wine should be stored in a way that does not require one to shuffle bottles around in order to get to the desired choice. For this reason, and for general convenience, it is important for collectors to consider their racking needs and plan accordingly. For those collectors who do not purchase wine by the case, diamond bins can be a nuisance, not to mention a potential danger to wine bottles. Installing single bottle racking will decrease the chances that bottles will be broken as a result of excessive rearranging and shuffling.

As always, good planning and smart habits will protect wine for years to come.

This incredible 7,000 bottle wine cellar features real stone flooring, a 17th century rug, and a sixteenth century school desk. Opposite page: Diamond racks define the front and back walls, framed by Texas limestone-block arches. An antique back bar and dining table add to the old world feel of a new home.

This wine cellar's rustic appeal is mixed with plenty of sophistication. Not one inch of storage space is lost, yet it escapes a claustrophobic feeling with loads of light, white flooring, and decorative openings with mirror backing. An arched doorway between two separate areas also gives the impression of space, while the table adds just the right amount of color. The antique grape press is a great decorative element.

The arched doorways and a tile floor with diamond accents give distinctive character to this refined wine cellar. The dark ceiling contrasts nicely with redwood and light-colored floor. Simple and elegant racking features curved corners and a display rack. Tables made from racking afford a great space for wine tasting and a smart way to store more wine.

Guests can enjoy a glass of wine while sitting at a glass-top table in the spacious and open wine cellar. Decorative openings filled with plants and bottles add character and depth. Opposite page: Glass doors open up to simple and stylish racking with curved corners. Distinctive quarter round shelves afford a great space to display and store large bottles.

Restaurant Marketing and Display

Display can pay. That's the lesson that restaurant owners and designers are learning. By creating an environment that announces a serious wine program, patrons are encouraged to consider wine more seriously as they select their entrees.

That's the message that Brian Yost, restaurant and beverage vice president for the enormous Marriott International chain of hotels and restaurants, emphasizes as he constantly works to refine the organization's wine list.

Wine display is as much form as it is function, says Yost. With a beautiful wine display—be it visible wine storage cabinets or a number of large-format wine bottles—the restaurant is making a statement that "this dining experience should include wine."

"We look for unique ways to make that statement," Yost said. "We view wine as integral to the dining experience. Every dinner should include wine. We'd like to see it come back for lunch, as well, but that's probably not going to happen in the near future."

Recent years have witnessed a tremendous growth in consumer interest in all types of beverages. Evidence of the increased interest in wine ranges from soaring readership of major wine publications, a weekly wine list in *Newsweek* magazine, and a reality television show based on life in a fine-dining restaurant. "The consumer is ripe," Yost said. "There's a real thirst for knowledge about, and experiences with, spirits."

Wine displays flank a fireplace and mantle decorated with a fisherman's portrait and prize catch in The Fish House, Toronto. Display emphasizes wine's importance to the dining experience.

"Experience" is a word Yost returns to with regularity, and wine is his favorite beverage.

"Wine tends to be the most romantic, and it has the most universal appeal," he said. "Wine sales, culturally, are a much higher percentage of sales than beer or cocktails."

Perhaps as a result, restaurants around the world are addressing the interest in wine.

"A wine cellar dining experience is just one more level of experience," Yost said. "The objective is to bring people back; to build repeat customers. To offer them the same quality experience, but maybe in a different manner. You can create programming that complements the integrity of the environment—organize a wine event paired with a wine expert, tasting events, or five-course meals paired with wines."

Some restaurants are offering tasting portions of wine, or establishing bar areas dedicated solely to wine. While these virtual altars to wine are at base a merchandising technique, savvy isn't enough to make a restaurant owner successful. Knowledge is critical, and staff training

The sleek, contemporary décor of this dining area in the Mustard Grille of Toronto is enriched by a "swinging" mural on the wall and faux grapevines hanging from the ceiling. Wine stored in diagonal bins behind glass cabinets tempts and inspires thirst.

comes increasingly important as guest expectations rise. The number one barrier to selling wine is lack of staff comfort, Yost said.

In any given restaurant, therefore, it is hoped that one or two people who work the bar will have a passion for wine that will help them become the experts and leaders of the restaurant wine program. At the upper end of the service chain, a restaurant may provide a wine steward or sommelier.

There are two types of sommelier, Yost suggests. One is the classically trained wine expert, who chooses wines for the guest that will best enhance the dining experience. This type of sommelier provides a very useful service in helping guests who want to learn or who need validation in their selections. The other kind of sommelier, Yost says, is the one who consults with guests. This sommelier or wine steward will quiz guests about what kind of wines they usually buy or drink, then will derive a direction from the guests' responses about recommendations to make. Not only are the recommendations of this inquisitive type of sommelier usually spot-on, says Yost, but this professional is growing and learning about consumer needs.

Double-sided racks in the window of Santa Monica's Third Street Deli entice passersby as well as customers. Blackout blinds protect the wine from the afternoon sun.

Over 3,000 bottles of wine are housed in this magnificent wine cellar, located in a medieval tower of the seventeenth century Palazzo Gori Pannilini in Sienna, Italy; also home to the Grand Hotel Continental. A visit to Sapordivino's wine cellar affords an experience that blends the classic and the avant-garde – a characteristic of Sapordivino's décor and wine selection. Bottles stored in glass racking seem to float along the ancient, rose-hued walls, as do the sleek, glass and metal stairways and passageways. The wine cellar may be visited by invitation only, or may be booked for private events and tastings.

Electric candelabras add soft elegance to this 12,000 bottle cellar. Other rich decorative details include flooring that looks like water, an arched doorway with decorative stained-glass window, and dark ceiling and walls that contrast decorously with the light-colored wood of racking. Windsor chairs create country ambiance for this cozy, glass-enclosed dining area within a wine cellar. Elegance and down home warmth mingle to form a distinctive combination.

Australia & New Zealand

Distressed timber frames the doorway to a wine cellar lined in schist stone – the ideal location for a comprehensive collection of New Zealand's finest vintages. The Wine Cave is provided for intimate parties of up to six people for dining or on-request wine tastings. There they are seated among award winning Pinot Noirs, Chardonnays, Sauvignon Blancs, and Rieslings, all grown and bottled in New Zealand.

Blanket Bay
PO Box 35
Glenorchy, New Zealand
+64 3 442 9442
www.blanketbay.com

Burswood International Resort and Casino
Great Eastern Highway
Burswood, Western Australia 6100
PO Box 500, Victoria Park WA 6979
+618 93 62 7777
www.burswood.com.au

Roberts on Tower Estate
Halls Road
Pokolbin NSW 2325
Australia
+02 49 98 7330
www.robertsatpeppertree.com.au
    In the heart of Australian wine country, Roberts on Tower Estate features a wine cellar stocked with a wide selection of premium wines from the Hunter Valley, together with wines from other Australian regions and around the world. Guests choose their wine straight from the rack when they dine here.

The Windows Wine Cellar at the Burswood International Resort in Australia is available for a private dining experience for up to twenty guests.

Canada

The Arlington Hotel
106 Grand River Street North
Paris, Ontario N3L 2M5
Canada
519-442-1019
877-833-9083
www.arlingtonhotelparis.com

The Arlington Hotel in Ontario offers an amazing wine cellar dining experience in their rustic wine cellar and cellar lounge. Visitors can listen to music while sipping fine vintages with complimentary cheese and bruschetta.

Jonathan's of Oakville
120 Thomas Street
Oakville, Ontario
L6J-3A8
905-842-4200
www.jonathansofoakville.com

The wine cellar dining room in Jonathan's of Oakville boasts one of the best and most diverse wine lists in Southern Ontario. The restaurant offers its cellar as an exclusive private room for small groups.

The Rimrock Resort Hotel
Mountain Avenue, P.O. Box 1110
Banff, Alberta, T1L 1J2
Canada
403-762-3356
www.rimrockresort.com

The wine cellar at the Rimrock Resort Hotel features over 500 fine wines and two sommeliers to assist in the choice of the perfect wine. See the cellar from the hotel's Classico Restaurant.

Sooke Harbour House
1528 Whiffen Spit Road
Sooke, British Columbia V0S 1N0
Canada
250-642-3421
www.sookeharbourbouse.com

The Sooke Harbour House's restaurant features award-winning cuisine and a wine selection that fluctuates between 2,500 and 2,800 wines. The wine list offers a great selection of British Columbia white, red, and dessert wines, in addition to a selection of wines from Ontario. Champagne and sparkling wine, German rieslings, chardonnays from Burgundy, white wines from California, and red wines from Australia, France, Italy, Washington, and California are other highlights of the wine list.

Europe

Hotel Viña del Mar Pineta
c.p. 222 - Via Oriente, 58
30017 Lido Di Jesolo, Venice
Italy
+39 042 196 1182
+39 042 136 2458
www.vinadelmar.it/enotecae.htm
Everyone is welcome to come visit the Hotel Viña del Mar Pineta's wine cellar to partake in a special tasting menu. Open May through October.

Nordic Hotels
Vasaplan Box 884
SE-101 37 Stockholm
Sweden
+46 850 56 3000
www.nordichotels.se
A visit to Stockholm offers a chance to visit the Nordic Light Hotel's modern wine cellar. Attend tastings of the cellar's collection of imported American wines organized by the Hotel's sommelier.

Oaks Hotel
Porlock, Exmoor
West Somerset TA24 8ES
United Kingdom
+16 43 86 2265
www.oakshotel.co.uk/index.htm
The Oaks Hotel Restaurant boasts a collection of over 100 wines. The hotel deals directly with shippers and growers such as Guigal, Louis Latour & Bouchard Pere et Fils in France, Weinart of Argentina, Concha y Torro & Cousina Macul of Chile, and Torres of Spain.

Restaurant René at the Hotel Ritz
Banegaardsplads 12
Århus 8000
Denmark
+45 86 13 4444
www.hotelritz.dk/engelsk
Restaurant René's wine cellar offers an experience out of the ordinary. 8,000 bottles are stored in more than three-and-a-half kilometers of iron shelves and span an impressive 150 years. The wine cellar has everything from old Madeira to the most recent Beaujolais wines, and an impressive collection of Chateau D'Yquem. The wine cellar offers large, private dining experiences.

United States

United States
'21' Club
21 West 52nd Street
New York, NY 10019
212-582-7200
www.21club.com

The exclusive, celebrity rich '21' Club in New York City became the place to be during Prohibition, and they've built a great career upon providing fine spirits and food to patrons willing to pay for it. The wine cellar was built to be invisible. Closeted behind several smoked hams that hung from the basement ceiling and a wall shelf filled with canned goods, stood a perfectly camouflaged 2-1/2 ton door. Only by inserting a slender 18-inch length of wire in one of the many cracks in the cement wall would the door silently slide back to reveal the '21's most coveted treasure: 2,000 cases of wine!

Today that peculiar door is still opened with a wire, revealing a series of rooms containing the restaurant's renowned wine collection and rare liquors. The rooms also house the the private collections of the some of the restaurant's most famous patrons, past and present, including Presidents Gerald Ford and Richard Nixon, Elizabeth Taylor, Governor Hugh Carey, Ivan Boesky, Eva Gabor, Aristotle Onassis, and Burgess Meredith. The cellar was recently remodeled

to create an opportunity to dine in an atmosphere steeped in history. The private dining area seats twenty patrons amidst wine racks. The booth in the corner was named for Jimmy Walker, the former New York City mayor who enjoyed a private booth in a corner of the cellar during Prohibition.

Ashley's Restaurant and Wine Cellar at the Sheraton Grand
4440 W. John Carpenter Freeway
Irving, TX 75063
972-929-8400
www.sheratongrandfw.com

Ashley's award-winning wine cellar offers a private setting for special occasions and accommodates up to six people.

Canoe Bay
P.O. Box 28
Chetek, WI 54728
715-924-4594
www.canoebay.com

Dedicated to red wines, the Canoe Bay wine cellar includes peek-a-boo windows to the inn hallway beyond. Couples may reserve the table for a unique and especially private dining experience. The Wine Cellar Dinner includes a sparkling wine aperitif, a full menu, and a glass of dessert wine. Ladies are advised to bring a shawl.

The Capital Hotel
Markham & Louisiana
Little Rock, AK 72201
501-374-7474
www.thecapitalhotel.com

 This hotel discreetly tucked its wine cellar beyond the kitchen and hotel laundry, with a secret entrance that recreates the allure of Prohibition era speakeasies. Yet the dining venue is entirely new, designed to accommodate private parties of 16-20 people. It is also a working wine cellar, with the temperature maintained to store the hotel's 600 spirit selections and 2,400 bottle wine list, recognized by *Wine Spectator* magazine with an Award of Excellence.

Cetrella Bistro and Café
845 Main Street
Half Moon Bay, CA 94019
650-726-4090
www.cetrella.com

Guests can dine in the company of more than 250 different wines and 50 different varietals. The private Wine Cellar Dining Room seats up to twenty guests around a large, cherry wood table imported from Italy. Cetrella's extensive award-winning international wine list was carefully selected to harmonize with the Northern Mediterranean cuisine and to complement selections from the European cheese room, located right outside the wine cellar. The restaurant offers ongoing wine classes and monthly five-course Wine Lover'sDinners, where guests learn about the pairing of food, wine and spirits.

Geiser Grand Hotel
1996 Main Street
Baker City, OR 97814
888-434-7374
541-523-1889
www.geisergrand.com

Oregon's Geiser Grand Hotel provides its wine cellar for meetings or banquets of up to forty people. The nineteenth-century rock walls with original doors and windows boast a unique charm.

The Forge in the Forest Restaurant
PO Box 6088
S.W. Corner of 5th and Junipero
Carmel, CA 93921
831-624-2233
www.forgeintheforest.com

This large, King Arthur style round table is reserved for intimate private parties and is situated under an enormous wrought iron chandelier hung from a domed ceiling of hand painted clouds framed by brick and neon. The cellar is bordered by large format bottles cradled in wrought iron racks against walls adorned with hand painted murals.

Hotel Bellwether
One Bellwether Way
Bellingham, WA 98225
877-411-1200
www.hotelbellwether.com
Up to sixteen people can be seated in these imported Louis XIV-style chairs in the European-style dining room and wine cellar of the Harborside Bistro Restaurant in the Hotel Bellwether. The mahogany-stained table is set with fine crystal glasses and an even finer selection of wine.

Hotel Monaco Denver
1717 Champa Street at 17th
Denver, CO 80202
800-990-1303
www.manaco-denver.com/html/dining.htm
Denver's Hotel Monaco offers private wine cellar dining for up to fifty guests.

Kuleto's Trattoria
1095 Rollins Road
Burlingame, CA 94010
650-342-4922
www.kimptongroup.com/kuleto_s_trattoria.html
Private dining available for up to 120 guests in the private wine cellars.

Lake Placid Lodge
P.O. Box 550
Lake Placid, NY 12946
518-523-2700
www.lakeplacidlodge.com
Resort president and woodworking hobbyist David W. Garrett created the handsome centerpiece for the wine cellar in his Lake Placid Lodge. He mounted a favorite painting within a cork and twig-inlaid credenza. Six-course wine cellar dinners are offered for two to eight guests, who choose their wine directly from the racks and assemble personalized menus in conjunction with the executive chefs. A souvenir wine glass goes home with each guest to this exclusive dining. The inn won an award of excellence from Wine Spectator, is on the Gold List of Condé Nast Traveler's best places to stay, and is listed among the top ten resorts with Zagat and Andrew Harper's Hidaway Resorts.

Lovell's of Lake Forest
915 S. Waukegan Road
Lake Forest, IL 60045
847-234-8013
www.lovellsoflakeforest.com/
 Lovell's of Lake Forest has an elegant wine cellar that can accommodate up to twelve people for intimate private gatherings.

The Mansion on Turtle Creek
2821 Turtle Creek Blvd.
Dallas, TX 75219
214-559-2100
www.mansiononturtlecreek.com
 The Wine Cellar in The Mansion on Turtle Creek is an intimate and elegant setting. Surrounded by warm, candle-lit ambiance, up to twelve guests are served meals on 24-carat gold china by an award-winning culinary staff and sommelier.

Masa's Restaurant
648 Bush Street
San Francisco, CA 94108
415-989-7154
800-258-7694
www.masas.citysearch.com

 The careful combination of decorative elements lends a ripe finish to Masa Restaurant's private dining room in San Francisco, California. Green upholstered chairs and coordinating flower pot filled with daffodils provide the perfect color accompaniment to the subdued tones of redwood racking and dark carpet with white lattice pattern. Decorative openings add excitement and depth to the space, while a variety of racking options add versatility.

Oceana Restaurant
55 East 54th Street
New York, NY 10022
212-759-5941
www.oceanarestaurant.com

   The wine cellar can accommodate up to twenty-four people, along with a large portion of the restaurant's fine collection of red wines. The "Wine Cellar Experience" begins with hors d'oeuvres passed butler-style, accompanied by an aperitif, followed by a seasonal degustation menu with specially selected wines to complement each course. The finale – a dessert extravaganza matched with lush dessert wines to bring the evening to a stellar close.

The Olde Greenfield Inn
595 Greenfield Road
Lancaster, PA
717-393-0668
www.theoldegreenfieldinn.com/

   Located in a 1780 Pennsylvania farmhouse, the Olde Greenfield Inn offers romantic dining in its wine cellar.

Pazzo Ristorante
621 SW Washington St
Portland,OR 97205
503-228-1515
http://www.pazzoristorante.citysearch.com

   Private dining available for up to sixty guests in the wine cellar.

Peabody Orlando Hotel
9801 International Drive
Orlando, FL 32819
407-352-4000
www.peabodyorlando.com/asp/home.asp

   The Peabody Hotel Orlando's magnificent exhibition wine cellar is visible from multiple dining rooms. It features transparent double-glazed doors and walls, brass trim, and state-of-the-art temperature and humidity controls.

The Peninsula Beverly Hills
9882 South Santa Monica Boulevard
Beverly Hills, CA 90212
310-551-2888
800-462-7899
www.fasttrack.beverlyhills.peninsula.com

The attractive walnut wine cellar of the Peninsula Hotel of Beverly Hills is coupled with the light and airy main dining room. A glass-paned doorway with molding elegantly separates the two rooms. Romantic décor and warm lighting display a feminine sensibility, while the handsomely decorated cellar with black marble flooring has a more masculine appeal. A match made in heaven!

Petroleum Club of Houston
800 Bell Street, 43rd Floor
Houston, TX 77002
713-659-1431
713-659-1281
www.pcoh.com

The Petroleum Club's Vintage Room can be reserved for meetings and parties, and provides seating for up to twenty-four people among displays of fine vintages.

The Pitcher Inn
275 Main Street
Warren, VT 05674
802-496-6350
888-867-4824
www.pitcherinn.com

The Pitcher Inn's wine cellar holds 6,500 bottles. One of Vermont's finest cellars, it boasts a private dining table that is available for an intimate dinner.

Rio All-Suite Hotel
3700 West Flamingo Road
Las Vegas, NV 89103-4046
702-777-7777
800-752-9746
http://riosuite.casinocity.com

The wine cellar showcases 50,000 bottles, with rare museum pieces and hard-to-find "cult wine" in special displays. Visitors should be sure not to miss the bottle of 1800 Madeira from the cellar of Thomas Jefferson, or the 1855 to 1990 vertical collection of Chateau d'Yquem, valued at 2 million dollars. The wine cellar at the Rio All-Suite Hotel is filled with highly collectable labels from around the world, such as Italy's Sassicia or Australia's Penfold's Grange. The wine bar offers 100 wines by the glass and a wine and food pairing menu. The Wine Cellar specializes in private wine tasting seminars as well as wine tasting parties and dinners.

Sardine Factory Wine Cellar
701 Wave Street
Monterey, CA 93940
831-373-3775
www.sardinefactory.com

The Sardine Factory's lavishly decorated wine cellar is carved into arched catacombs. Wrought-iron gates separate the wine vaults from the dining area, adorned with sixteenth century antiques. The twenty-five-foot banquet table, made from a single piece of Big Sur redwood, seats up to twenty-eight guests and is set with candelabra and fine china. Exquisite food and wine, a richly intimate ambiance, white glove service, and music marry to form this wine cellar dining experience reserved exclusively for private parties.

Sun Mountain Lodge
PO Box 1000
Winthrop, WA 98862
509-996-2211
www.sunmountainlodge.com

Sun Mountain Lodge's wine cellar contains one of the most extensive resort wine collections in the Pacific Northwest, with over 5,000 bottles and 450 different labels. The cellar has an outstanding collection of Northwest and California wines, as well as many others from around the globe. Opened in 1998, the cellar was designed to mirror the classic cave cellars of Europe. Designed by NBBJ of Seattle, it features stone and ironwork by local craftsmen, as well as a large cherry wood dining table with seating for fourteen.

The Sutton Place Hotel
4500 MacArthur Boulevard
Newport Beach, CA 92660
949-476-2001
www.suttonplace.com

One of the world's largest private collections of Bordeaux – including Château Lafite-Rothschild, Mouton Rothschild, Margaux, Latour, Haut Brion, and d'Yquem, and an extensive line of rare Pétrus – is on display during private wine cellar dinner parties at The Sutton Place Hotel. Though the cellar cooling systems are temporarily reduced for private functions, the temperature remains cool to preserve the invaluable collection. More than 20,000 bottles witness these exclusive events. The true celebrities at any gathering are the rare and highly valued vintages lounging upon the Philippine mahogany racks, including a case of Heitz, Martha's Vinyard, 1974 – arguably one of the best wines ever produced from California and recently named to *Wine Spectator's* "Wines of the Century" list. Other rare wines include Château Latour, 1945, named the "Vintage of the Century;" Roederer, Cristal, 1990; Château d'Yquem, 1988 and 1990, and a Château Pétrus Impérial, 1989, signed by Christian Moueix.

White Barn Inn
37 Beach Avenue
Kennebunkport, ME 04046
207-967-2321
http://www.whitebarninn.com/

The Wine Room at the White Barn Inn offers an elegant and unique atmosphere for private dining events of ten to fourteen guests. The cellar stores up to 7,000 bottles of hand-picked wines. It features a custom dining table of imported Indian granite surrounding a wraparound black leather banquette. Mahogany and red cedar wine casements are enhanced by a specially commissioned mural by local artist Judith Hardenbrook depicting the lush countryside of Tuscany. An antiqued Italian chiaro marble floor and soft lighting give a nice finish to the warm and rustic décor.

Additional Wine Cellar Resources

Gold, Richard M. *How and Why to Build a Wine Cellar*. North Amherst: Sandhill Publishing, 2002.

Gollnek, Olaf and Dirk Meyhofer. *The Architecture of Wine*. Corte Madera: Gingko Press, 2000.

Stelzer, Tyson. *Cellaring Wine: Do-it-Yourself Solutions. Wine Press,* 2002.

Immer, Andrea. *Great Wine Made Simple : Straight Talk from a Master Sommelier. New York: Broadway Books, 2000.*

www.intowine.com. This website is managed by the M2 Wine Education Center, and provides lots of useful information about wine.

www.stratsplace.com/how_cellmiked.html. Contains images of an entirely passive cellar in a private home and details of the cellar's construction.

www.vinote.com. Vinoté sells wine cellaring software and its website offers useful information for cellaring novices and experts, including a section about wine books.

www.wineloverspage.com. Visit this website's discussion forums for advice on the best wines and helpful tips for constructing a wine cellar.

www.winereader.com. A comprehensive website dedicated to providing enophiles with directories to wine magazines, websites, and books. A free newsletter is also provided.

www.wineontheweb.com/index.html. A talking wine magazine on the web, offering consumer advice and interesting news in the wine world. Also contains a comprehensive links page for wine resources.

Contributors

Apex Wine Cellars

13221 Northup Way, Bellevue, WA 98005

425-644-1178, 800-462-2714

www.apexwinecellars.com

American Wine Essentials, Inc.

1472 N. Milpitas Blvd., Milpitas, CA 95035

877-719-8486

www.amwe.com

California Redwood Association

405 Enfrente Drive, Suite 200, Novato, CA 94949-7206

415-382-0662

www.calredwood.org

Harrison Design Associates

3198 Cains Hill Place, NW Suite 200, Atlanta, GA 30305

404-365-7760

www.harrisondesignassociates.com

Harrison Design California, Inc.

921 St. Vincent Ave., Santa Barbara, CA 93101

805-899-3434

www.harrisondesignassociates.com

Hirschberg Design Group, Inc.

334 Queen Street E., Toronto, Ontario M5A 1S8, Canada

416-868-1210

www.hirschbergdesign.com

MasterBrand Cabinets, Inc.

1 MasterBrand Cabinets Dr., Jasper, IN 47546

812-482-2527

www.mbcabinets.com

Paul Wyatt Designs: Fine Wine Rack and Cellar Company

512 Technology Way, Napa, CA 94558

701-251-8463

www.fine-wine.com; www.paulwyatt.com; www.finewinerack.com

Robert Wood and Sons

Stone Art Work, 6216 S. Wildman Lane, Coeur d'Alene, ID 83814

208-667-7705

www.stoneartwork.com

Rosehill Wine Cellars, Inc.

339 Olivewood Road, Toronto, Ontario M8Z 2Z6 Canada

888-253-6807, 416-285-6604

www.rosehillwinecellars.com

Sapordivino Winebar & Restaurant

Grand Hotel Continental, Banchi di Sopra 85, 53100 Siena, Italy

+39 05 775 60 11

www.ghcs.com

Valentini's Custom Wine Cellars

P.O. Box 94435, Las Vegas, NV 89193

888-330-6371

www.worldclasscellars.com

Viking Range Corporation

111 Front Street, Greenwood, MS 38930

888-VIKING1 (845-4641)

www.vikingrange.com

The Wine Enthusiast

103 Fairview Park Drive, Elmsford, NY 10523

800-356-8466

www.wineenthusiast.com

WineRacks.com

P.O. Box 67, High Falls, NY 12440

888-687-2517

www.wineracks.com

Wood Mode Custom Cabinetry

One Second Street, Kreamer, PA 17833

800-635-7500

www.wood-mode.com

Photo Credits

Rather than just a space for storage, wine cellars provide the opportunity to escape to another land through creative design elements. The hand-painted faux-stone arches built from drywall add texture and character to the room. The countertop is made of granite. A ceiling strung with faux grapevines gives the impression of walking through a Tuscan vineyard.

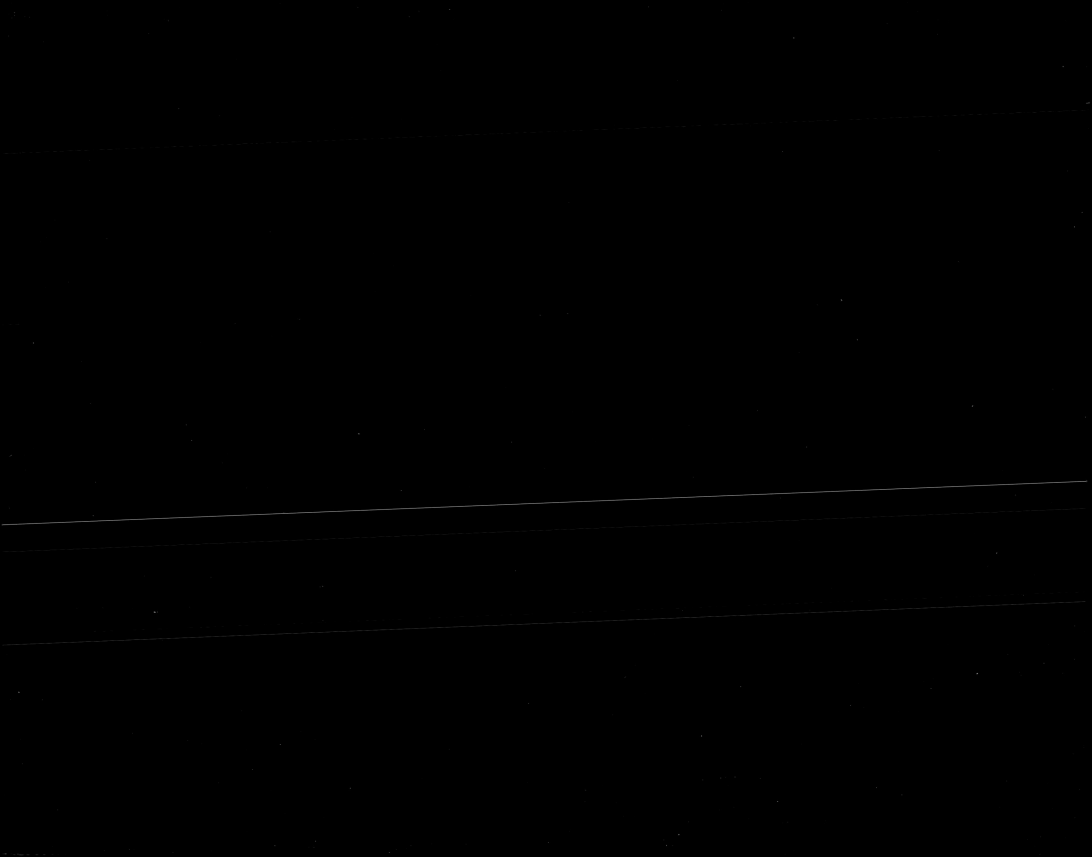

USA $49.95

ISBN: 0-7643-1965-5